Contents

Key: *easy **medium ***difficult

Some words are shown in bold, **like this**. You can find out what they mean by looking in the glossary.

Being vegetarian

The word **vegetarian** was first used in England in 1847. It describes a diet that includes no meat or poultry. Most vegetarians avoid seafood too. Very strict vegetarians are called **vegans**. They do not eat anything that comes from animals, including honey, eggs, or milk.

Why be vegetarian?

There are many reasons why a person might choose to be a vegetarian. Sometimes people cannot afford to buy meat. Families might keep cows or chickens for milk and eggs, but their animals are too valuable to kill.

Some people feel that killing animals is cruel and so they refuse to eat meat. Other people feel that raising animals for food uses too many of the Earth's resources. It takes fewer resources to raise plant crops than to raise animals for food. Raising cattle for beef requires huge amounts of maize and grain. It also causes soil erosion and uses a great deal of water.

Being vegetarian is sometimes a religious choice. Followers of the Hindu religion in India believe that all life, including animal life, is sacred (holy). Hindus believe in non-violence to animals. Buddhist monks usually do not eat meat. Sikhs serve vegetarian food at religious ceremonies. Some Roman Catholics do not eat meat during Lent, the weeks before Easter.

Vegetarian nutrition

The vegetarian diet is very healthy. It is low in fats but high in fibre and **vitamins**. However, meat and animal products (milk, cheese, eggs, yoghurt) are high in **protein**. To make sure they eat enough protein, vegetarians eat foods such as beans. Tofu, made from soya beans, can be used instead of meat in some recipes. To have a balanced diet, vegetarians eat a wide range of cereal grains, vegetables, seeds, nuts, and fruits.

Around the world

There are more **vegetarians** today than there have ever been, and their numbers are growing.

Is it healthy to be a vegetarian?

Animal foods, such as meat, fish, and eggs, contain **protein**, which our bodies need to stay healthy. Fruit, **pulses** and, vegetables do not have as much protein as animal foods, but eating a good range of them will give you all the protein you need.

A wide variety of vegetables is sold in India.

The vegetarian world

There are vegetarians in every part of the world. The recipes in this book come from all around the world. The map below shows you the countries where the recipes in this book come from.

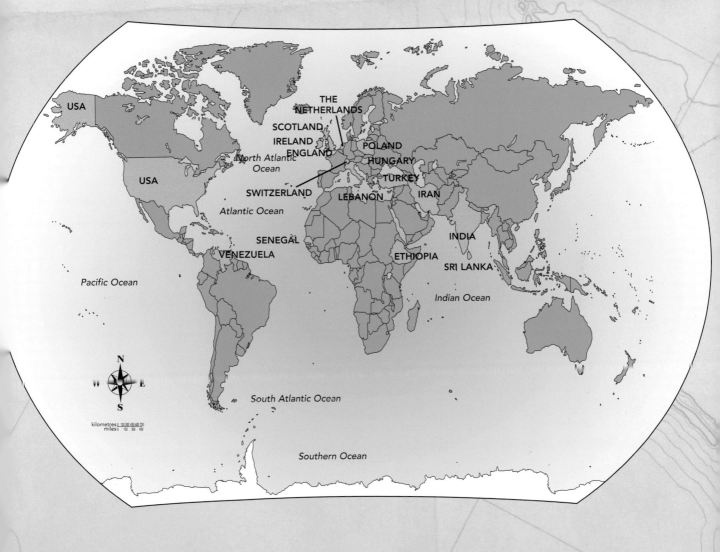

USA

THE NETHERLANDS

SCOTLAND

IRELAND

ENGLAND

POLAND

HUNGARY

North Atlantic Ocean

USA

SWITZERLAND

TURKEY

LEBANON

IRAN

Atlantic Ocean

SENEGAL

VENEZUELA

ETHIOPIA

INDIA

SRI LANKA

Pacific Ocean

Indian Ocean

South Atlantic Ocean

Southern Ocean

kilometres 0 150 300 450 600 750
miles 0 150 300 450

Vegetarian food

Many people in the world are **vegetarian**. This means that they do not eat any meat. Some vegetarians eat fish, but no meat. Other vegetarians, called **vegans**, do not eat any food that has come from an animal, including milk and eggs. Instead of dairy products, they may eat foods made with soya milk, from soya beans. Whatever people eat, it is important to make sure that their body is getting the **nutrients** it needs.

Here are some examples of the foods vegetarians eat to have a varied diet and stay healthy.

squash

cabbage

pineapple

swede

lemon

red peppers

peas

yoghurt

potatoes

carrots

sweetcorn

apples

onion

turnips

garlic

ginger

cheese

bread

beans

leeks

cinnamon

Pulses

Pulses are beans, and seeds from plants. They include broad beans, black-eyed beans and chick peas. Pulses are a very good source of **protein** and can be cooked in many different ways. You can buy most pulses dried or tinned.

Nuts

Nuts, such as walnuts, pecan nuts, and peanuts, are another good source of protein. Many cooking styles around the world use nuts in sweet and savoury recipes. Nuts contain quite a lot of fat, so do not eat too many.

Dairy or soya products

Milk, cheese, and yoghurt are dairy products. They contain protein and **calcium**, which help to give us strong bones and teeth. Vegans can get calcium from dairy substitutes, such as soya milk with added calcium. Supermarkets sell both types of products.

Fruit and vegetables

Fruit and vegetables are a good source of **vitamins**, which everyone needs to stay healthy. You can buy many different kinds of fruit and vegetables in supermarkets and grocery shops. They come from all over the world. Dried fruit, and canned and frozen fruit and vegetables, contain nutrients, too.

Cereals

More people in the world eat rice every day than any other food. It is a **staple** ingredient in many countries. People also eat other cereals, such as wheat and barley. Health food shops sell a variety of grains, including bulgur wheat.

Before you start

Which recipe should I try?

The recipes you choose to make depends on many things. Some recipes make a good main course, while others are better as starters. Some are easy, others are more difficult.

The top right-hand page of each recipe has information that can help you. It tells you how long each recipe will take and how many people it serves. You can multiply or divide the quantities if you want to cook for more or fewer people. This section also shows how difficult each dish is to make: the recipes are easy (*), medium (**), or difficult (***) to cook. The symbols in the corner can help you quickly find certain recipes. Here is a key that will help you.

Healthy choice: These recipes are healthy to eat.

Quick and easy: These recipes are quick and easy to make.

Sweet treat: These recipes make a good dessert or sweet snack.

This symbol is sign of a dangerous step in a recipe. For these steps, take extra care or ask an adult to help.

Kitchen rules

There are a few basic rules you should always follow when you cook:

- Ask an adult if you can use the kitchen.
- Wash your hands before you start.
- Wear an apron to protect your clothes. Tie back long hair.
- Be very careful when using sharp knives.
- Never leave pan handles sticking out – it could be dangerous if you bump into them.
- Always wear oven gloves to lift things in and out of the oven.
- Wash fruit and vegetables before you use them.

Quantities and measurements

Ingredients for recipes can be measured in two different ways. Metric measurements use grams, litres, and millilitres. Imperial measurements use cups, ounces, and fluid ounces. In the recipes in this book you will see the following abbreviations:

tbsp = tablespoons   oz = ounces

tsp = teaspoons   ml = millilitres

g = grams   cm = centimetres

Utensils

To cook the recipes in this book, you will need these utensils, as well as kitchen essentials, such as spoons, plates, and bowls.

- 18cm flan case
- 18cm plate
- apple corer
- baking sheets
- **colander**
- **fish slice**
- food processor or blender
- grater
- heatproof bowl
- kitchen spatula
- large frying pan
- lemon squeezer
- measuring jug
- ovenproof dish
- pastry brush
- plastic or glass chopping board (easier to clean than wooden ones)
- potato masher
- rolling pin
- set of scales
- sharp knife
- sieve
- slotted spoon
- small and large saucepans, with lids
- tea towel
- whisk

Broad bean pâté with ciabatta toast (Italy)

There are many **vegetarian** recipes from Italy. This one is from Tuscany, an area famous both for its old towns and cities, and for its beautiful countryside. This recipe uses frozen broad beans, because fresh ones are only available for a short time each year. Ciabatta (pronounced *chee-a-batta*) is a type of Italian bread, which you can find in many supermarkets or bakeries. Serve the pâté with some salad as an ideal starter, light lunch, or snack.

What you need

- 1 onion
- 3 garlic cloves
- 2 tbsp olive oil
- 400g frozen broad beans
- 70g reduced-fat cream cheese
- 1 lemon
- 1 ciabatta loaf

What you do

1 **Peel** and finely **chop** the onion and garlic.

 **2** Heat the oil in a small frying pan over a medium heat. **Fry** the onion and garlic for 5 minutes, until they are softened. Leave them to **cool**.

 **3** Put the frozen broad beans into a saucepan and cover them with water. Bring the water to the **boil**, **cover** the pan, and **simmer** the beans for 5 minutes.

4 **Drain** the beans and let them cool down.

5 Put them into a food processor or blender. Add the cream cheese and the fried onion mixture.

6 Cut the lemon in half. Using a lemon squeezer, squeeze the juice from both halves.

7 Add the lemon juice to the bean mixture, and **blend** until smooth.

8 Using a spatula, scrape the pâté into a bowl for serving.

9 **Slice** the ciabatta into pieces 2cm thick. **Grill** the slices of bread on each side, until lightly browned.

10 Serve the ciabatta warm with the pâté and some salad.

13

walnut, fenugreek, and yoghurt soup (Iran)

For hundreds of years, Iran was in the middle of trading routes between Europe and Asia. Iran's cooking style has been influenced by the many different people who have visited the country throughout history. In Iran, this soup is served hot or cold, as a starter or light lunch. It contains the **ground** seeds of a plant called fenugreek. Fenugreek leaves can be added to salads, too.

What you need

- 1 onion
- 1 tbsp vegetable oil or butter
- 50g walnuts
- 1 tsp ground fenugreek
- 600ml water
- 1 tbsp cornflour
- 500ml natural yoghurt

What you do

1 **Peel** and finely **chop** the onion.

2 Heat the oil or butter in a saucepan over a medium heat. Add the onion and **fry** over a medium to low heat for 4–5 minutes, until it has softened.

3 Put the walnuts into a blender, and **blend** until finely chopped. Add the walnuts and fenugreek to the saucepan.

4 In a bowl, stir 4 tbsp of the water into the cornflour.

5 Add the rest of the water to the pan. **Cover** and **simmer** for 20 minutes, and then allow to **cool** for 5 minutes.

6 Stir the yoghurt into the cornflour mixture. Add 240ml of the liquid from the saucepan to the yoghurt mixture, and stir well.

7 Slowly pour the yoghurt mixture into the pan, stirring all the time. Reheat the soup, but do not let it **boil**. Serve hot or cold with some bread.

MAKING YOGHURT

To make your own yoghurt, heat 500ml of milk until it is just boiling. Let it cool until it is warm, then stir in 2 tbsp plain natural yoghurt. Pour into a clean jar and keep in a warm place for 6–8 hours, until set. Chill the yoghurt for 12 hours before serving.

Black-eyed bean cakes (Ethiopia)

Farmers in north and central African countries, such as Ethiopia, grow black-eyed beans, or black-eyed peas, as they are sometimes called. African cooks usually soak the beans, pour them into a bowl, and **mash** them with a simple stone or wooden tool. They **deep-fry** their bean cakes, but in this version the cakes are fried in a little oil.

What you need

200g dried
    black-eyed beans
150g sweet potato
1 onion
Salt
Half a red chilli
    (optional)
1 tbsp flour
3 tbsp oil

What you do

1 Put the black-eyed beans into a bowl, and cover them with cold water. Leave them to soak overnight.

2 **Drain** the beans. Rub them between your hands so that the skins loosen. Put them into a bowl and cover them with water. Tip the water and skins away.

3 **Peel** the sweet potato and cut it into 2 cm chunks. Peel and finely **chop** the onion.

 4 Put the potato into a saucepan, cover it with **boiling** water, and add a pinch of salt. Cook for 15 minutes, or until it is tender, and then drain it.

 5 Cut the half-chilli in half lengthways and throw away the seeds. Chop the chilli finely. Wash your hands thoroughly after handling chilli. The juice can make your eyes and skin very sore.

Ready to eat: next day (including time to soak the beans).
Difficulty: ***. Serves 4.

6 Put the beans into a blender. Add the onion and chilli, and **blend** until smooth. Add the potato and blend again.

7 **Sprinkle** a little of the flour on to a work surface. Take out 2 tbsp of the mixture, and shape it into a ball. Then flatten it into a fritter shape. Do this with the rest of the mixture, to make about 20 fritters.

 8 Heat the oil in a large frying pan over a medium heat. **Fry** the bean cakes, four or five at a time, for 4 minutes on each side, until golden. Lift the cooked bean cakes on to kitchen paper.

9 Serve straight away, with cooked, green vegetables or salad, as a starter or light lunch.

Vegetarian shepherd's pie (England)

Shepherd's pie is traditionally made with minced lamb, which is high in fat, especially fats known as saturates, which are bad for health. This **vegetarian** version uses mixed beans instead of lamb. Beans are low in fat but still provide plenty of **protein** and other important **nutrients**. Beans are also a good source of fibre so they are filling and good for the digestive system.

What you need

700g potatoes
1 carrot
1 leek
1 clove of garlic
1 onion
1 tbsp vegetable oil
150ml semi-skimmed milk
50g hard cheese
420g canned mixed beans
400g canned chopped tomatoes
1 tsp dried mixed herbs
1 tsp tomato purée
3 tbsp water
Salt and pepper

What you do

 1 Wash and **peel** the potatoes and cut them into chunks. Cook them in a pan of **boiling** water until tender.

2 Prepare the other vegetables while the potatoes are cooking. Scrub the carrot and **dice** it. Cut off the green part and the root of the leek, split the leek in half, wash it carefully, and **slice** it. Crush the garlic. Peel the onion and **chop** it finely. **Drain** and **rinse** the beans.

Preheat the oven to 180°C/350°F/gas mark 4.

  Heat the oil in a large frying pan over a medium heat. **Fry** the onion until it is soft. Add the rest of the chopped vegetables and fry them for 10 minutes.

 Add the beans, tomatoes, herbs, tomato purée, and water to the frying pan. Stir thoroughly, **season**, and **simmer** the mixture for 5 minutes.

 While the mixture is simmering, **grate** the cheese.

Drain the potatoes. Heat the milk, taking care that it doesn't boil over. Pour it over the potatoes and **mash** until smooth, mixing in half the cheese.

Spoon the beans and tomato mixture into an ovenproof dish and top with the cheesy mash. **Sprinkle** over the remaining cheese.

Bake in the oven for 20 minutes, or until the topping is golden brown.

Barley and vegetable soup (Poland)

Winters in Poland can be extremely cold, so warm, filling soups such as this one are a popular lunch or supper dish. Polish farmers grow the vegetables this soup contains, as well as many different kinds of fruit. They bottle fruit or make it into jam, before **exporting** it to other countries.

What you need

75g pearl barley

1.5 litres hot water

1 carrot

1 parsnip

2 potatoes

1 celery stick

2 onions

2 tbsp vegetable oil

50g button mushrooms

2 vegetable stock cubes

Salt and pepper

What you do

1 Put the pearl barley into a bowl and cover it with cold water. Leave it to soak for 4 hours.

2 **Drain** the barley. Put it into a pan, add half the hot water, and bring it to the **boil. Cover** the pan and **simmer** for 30 minutes.

3 **Peel** the carrot and parsnip, and trim off both ends. Peel the potatoes.

4 **Dice** all three vegetables.

5 Trim the ends off the celery. **Slice** it into 1cm pieces.

6 Peel and **chop** the onions.

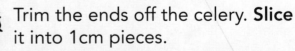

Ready to eat: 5¼ hours (including 4 hours for soaking the barley).
Difficulty: **. Serves 4.

7 Heat the oil in a large saucepan over a medium heat. **Fry** the onion for 3 minutes, or until it is softened. Add the celery, potato, carrot, and parsnip. Stir well and cook for 5 minutes, stirring occasionally.

8 Slice the mushrooms thinly and add them to the pan.

9 Add the pearl barley and the liquid it cooked in. Pour in the rest of the hot water.

10 Crumble the stock cubes into the pan, stirring well. Bring to the boil, cover, and simmer for 20 minutes.

11 **Season** the soup and spoon it into bowls. Serve with crusty bread.

Chick peas with sugar snap peas (Senegal)

Many traditional African dishes are made in one pot, hung over a fire. All the ingredients are cooked together as a complete meal, as in this recipe from Senegal, in north-west Africa. Sugar snap peas are grown throughout Africa.

What you need

1 onion

1 clove of garlic

450g sugar snap peas

2 tomatoes

1 tbsp vegetable oil

1 tsp black mustard seeds

1 tsp **ground** cumin

400g canned chick peas

What you do

 1 **Peel** and finely **chop** the onion and garlic.

 2 Cut the ends off the sugar snap peas. Cut the sugar snap peas in half.

3 Chop the tomatoes.

 4 Heat the oil in a medium saucepan over a medium heat. Add the onion and garlic, and **fry** for 3 minutes, or until they are softened.

 5 Stir in the sugar snap peas and tomatoes and cook for 5 minutes.

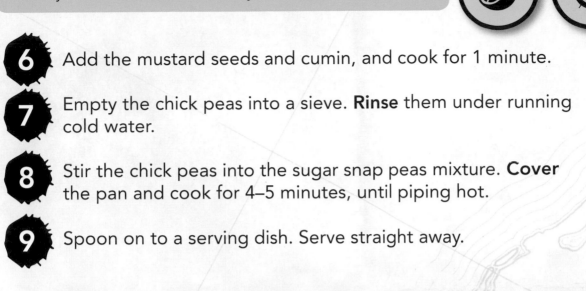

6 Add the mustard seeds and cumin, and cook for 1 minute.

7 Empty the chick peas into a sieve. **Rinse** them under running cold water.

8 Stir the chick peas into the sugar snap peas mixture. **Cover** the pan and cook for 4–5 minutes, until piping hot.

9 Spoon on to a serving dish. Serve straight away.

Colcannon (Ireland)

For centuries, potatoes were a **staple** food in Ireland. If the potato harvest failed, many people starved. Colcannon is a traditional dish that mixes potatoes with spring onions and cabbage. If it is served at Halloween, a silver coin or charm is sometimes stirred into the mixture – whoever gets the charm is supposed to marry within a year.

What you need

750g potatoes

Salt

Half a bunch of spring onions

100g cabbage

100ml semi-skimmed milk

50g butter

What you do

1 **Peel** the potatoes and cut them into 4cm chunks. Put them into a pan with a pinch of salt.

2 **Cover** the potatoes with **boiling** water. Bring the water back to the boil, cover, and **simmer** the potatoes until they are tender.

3 Trim the ends off the spring onions and throw them away. Thinly **slice** the spring onions.

4 Wash the cabbage and slice it thinly into small pieces.

5 Add the onions and the cabbage to the potatoes in the pan, and cook for a further 3 minutes.

6 Carefully **drain** the potatoes, onions, and cabbage into a **colander**, and then put them back into the hot pan.

7 **Mash** the vegetables with a potato masher. Add enough milk to make a light, fluffy mixture.

8 Stir in half the butter and **season** the mixture.

9 Put the colcannon into a serving dish. Make several dips in the top with a teaspoon and put a little bit of the rest of the butter into each dip. Serve hot, with other vegetables.

Olive, pomegranate, and walnut salad (Turkey)

Summers are very hot in Turkey, so people there usually eat a light lunch. They eat their main meal in the evening, when it is cooler. This recipe is from south-eastern Turkey, where farmers grow all the ingredients – olives, walnuts, and pomegranates.

What you need

1 pomegranate
50g fresh coriander
1 bunch of spring onions
120g walnuts
25g fresh sorrel or spinach leaves
120g Queen green olives

For the dressing:
3 tbsp olive oil
1½ tbsp lemon juice
Salt and pepper

What you do

1 Cut the pomegranate in half. Hold each half skin-side up over a bowl, and tap it with a rolling pin so that the seeds drop into the bowl.

2 **Chop** the coriander finely.

3 Trim the ends off the spring onions and throw them away. Thinly **slice** the spring onions.

4 Put the walnuts into a blender and **blend** until they are roughly chopped.

5 **Rinse** the sorrel or spinach leaves under running cold water, and pat them dry with a clean tea towel. Cut off the tough stalks.

6 Put the olive oil, lemon juice, and salt and pepper into a small screw-topped jar.

7 **Toss** all the salad ingredients together in a bowl. Shake the **dressing** well, pour it over the salad, and toss again.

8 Spoon the salad on to individual plates, and serve with crusty bread.

OLIVES

Olives grow on trees in groups called groves. Some olive trees can produce olives for up to 300 years. The olives are harvested and soaked in salt water for eating, or crushed to make olive oil.

Sweetcorn, pepper, and pumpkin stew (Venezuela)

Cooking all the ingredients for a meal in the same pot is part of traditional cooking in Venezuela, South America. Serve this vegetable stew as a main meal with crusty bread or rice.

What you need

2 onions

1 clove of garlic

400g pumpkin or butternut squash

2 corns on the cob, **thawed** if frozen

4 tomatoes

1 red pepper

4 medium-sized potatoes

2 tbsp vegetable oil

100g peas, fresh or frozen

1 tbsp chopped fresh marjoram

450ml water

Salt and pepper

What you do

1 **Peel** and finely **chop** the onions and garlic.

2 Peel the pumpkin or butternut squash, throw away the seeds, and cut the flesh into 2cm chunks.

3 If using fresh corns on the cob, pull the leaves and silky threads off.

4 Cut the tomatoes into quarters. Cut the pepper in half, and throw away the stalk and seeds. Cut the flesh into 3 cm pieces.

5 Peel the potatoes and cut them into 2 cm chunks.

6 Heat the oil in a flameproof casserole dish or large pan over a medium heat. **Fry** the onion for 3 minutes, add the garlic, and fry for 1 minute more.

7 Add the rest of the prepared vegetables, marjoram, and water to the pan. **Cover** and **simmer** for 25–30 minutes.

8 Using a slotted spoon, lift the sweetcorn on to a board. When it is **cool**, **slice** it into pieces 1cm thick.

9 Add the sweetcorn and peas to the pan, and cook for 5 minutes.

10 **Season** and stir the stew, and serve hot.

Tabbouleh (Lebanon)

Lebanon is in the Middle East, between Israel and Syria. Tabbouleh is a traditional Lebanese recipe, but people all over the Middle East make it. They may change some of the ingredients, depending on what is available locally, but it always includes bulgur wheat. Serve it with **pitta bread** or with other dishes, as a side salad.

What you need

175g bulgur (or cracked) wheat

550ml boiling water

1 lemon

2 tbsp olive oil

A quarter of a cucumber

2 spring onions

6 cherry tomatoes

4 tbsp chopped fresh parsley

2 tbsp chopped fresh mint

Salt and pepper

What you do

1 Put the bulgur wheat into a heatproof bowl. Pick out any small stones.

2 Pour the **boiling** water over the wheat and stir well. Leave it for 30 minutes, stirring from time to time.

3 Put a sieve over the sink and **drain** the wheat.

4 Cut the lemon in half. Using a lemon squeezer, squeeze the juice from both halves.

5 Stir the lemon juice and olive oil into the bulgur wheat.

6 **Dice** the cucumber into 1cm cubes.

7 Trim the ends off the spring onions. Cut the spring onions into 1cm slices.

8 Cut the cherry tomatoes in half. Stir the chopped herbs and tomatoes into the bulgur wheat with the cucumber. Add some salt and pepper.

9 Serve straight away, with pitta bread or crusty bread, or keep it in the fridge. (It will keep for up to 2 days.)

Winter vegetable goulash (Hungary)

In Hungary, winters are very cold and few things grow. This warming stew is made with winter vegetables, canned tomatoes, and a mild, red spice called paprika. Goulash can also have beans or meat as its main ingredient. Serve it as a main dish, with rice, pasta, or crusty bread.

What you need

2 onions

2 carrots

2 parsnips

200g swede

100g turnip

2 tbsp vegetable oil

300ml boiling water

1 tbsp paprika

2 tbsp plain flour

8 small new potatoes

400g canned chopped tomatoes

1 vegetable stock cube

2 tsp cornflour

2 tbsp cold water

142ml pot soured cream

2 tbsp chopped fresh parsley

What you do

1 **Peel** and finely **chop** the onions.

2 Peel and **slice** the carrots and parsnips.

3 Peel the swede and turnip. Cut them into slices 2cm thick, then into 2cm chunks.

4 Heat the oil in a large saucepan. Add the onions and **fry** them for 3 minutes, until softened.

 5 Stir in the chopped-up vegetables and paprika, and cook for 5 minutes, stirring from time to time.

 6 **Sprinkle** the flour over the vegetables and cook for 1 minute, stirring all the time.

 7 Pour the **boiling** water over the vegetables. Add the potatoes and tomatoes.

8 Crumble the stock cube over the pan and stir well. **Cover** and **simmer** for 25 minutes.

9 In a cup, mix the cornflour with the cold water. Stir the mixture into the soured cream, and then stir the cream into the vegetable mixture.

10 Carefully spoon the hot goulash into a serving dish, and sprinkle with parsley to serve.

Vegetable Cornish pasties (England)

Cornwall is in the far south-west of England. These filled pastry envelopes, called pasties, were first made as lunch for miners working deep in the Cornish tin-mines. The men could not wash their hands before eating, so they held a pastry corner as they ate, then threw away the dirty bit. They are ideal as part of a picnic or as a lunch.

What you need

125g potatoes

125g carrots

125g swede

Half a vegetable stock cube

1 onion

1 tbsp vegetable oil

1 tbsp flour

500 g packet ready-made shortcrust pastry

1 egg

What you do

1 **Peel** the potatoes, carrots, and swede. **Dice** these vegetables and put them into a saucepan.

2 Crumble the half stock cube into the saucepan and cover the vegetables with **boiling** water. Bring the water back to the boil and cook for 10 minutes.

3 Peel and finely **chop** the onion. Heat the oil in a small pan, and **fry** the onion over a low to medium heat for 4 minutes.

4 **Drain** the potato, swede, and carrots, and then add them to the onion. Leave them to **cool** completely.

5 **Preheat** the oven to 220°C/400°F/gas mark 6. **Sprinkle** the flour on to a work surface. Use a rolling pin to roll the pastry out until it is about 3mm thick.

Put an 18cm plate on the pastry and cut around it. Repeat this to make six pastry circles.

 Spoon the vegetables along the centre of each circle. Keep them away from the edge.

 Brush a little water around the circles' edges. Fold the pastry over the filling. Press the pastry edge between your fingers to make a zig-zag ridge along the edge of each pasty.

 Put the pasties on a baking tray. **Beat** the egg and brush a little over each pasty.

10 **Bake** for 25 minutes, until golden. Let the pasties cool a little before eating them.

Pineapple curry (Sri Lanka)

Sri Lanka is an island in the Indian Ocean, just off the southern tip of India. This recipe uses pineapples and coconuts, two of the island's main crops. It also uses the dried leaves of the curry plant, which add a spicy flavour. Use a heavy-based saucepan for this recipe, if you can. Sri Lankan cooks use a pot called a chatty.

What You need

A quarter of a fresh chilli (optional)

1 tsp mustard seeds

1 shallot

1 large, ripe pineapple

A quarter of a stem of lemon grass

1 tbsp vegetable oil

3 dried curry leaves

100ml reduced-fat coconut milk

A pinch of saffron

1 small cinnamon stick

½ tsp **ground** cumin

What You do

1  **Chop** the quarter chilli finely (if you are using it), and then wash your hands thoroughly. Chilli juice can make your eyes and skin very sore.

2 Put the mustard seeds into a small frying pan, and **toast** them over a medium heat for 30 seconds, until they pop. Tip them on to a plate.

3 **Peel** and finely chop the shallot.

4 Cut the pineapple in half. Cut off the thick skin and leaves, and throw them away. Cut out the tough core in the middle, and throw it away. Chop the flesh into 2cm chunks.

5 Peel off the outer leaves off the lemon grass. Trim off the root end and throw it away. Finely chop the lemon grass.

6 Heat the oil in a saucepan over a medium heat. **Fry** the shallot for 1 minute. Add the lemon grass and curry leaves, and fry for 1 minute.

7 Stir in the coconut milk and all the other ingredients, except the cumin. **Simmer** for 10 minutes, stirring from time to time.

8 Stir in the cumin, and simmer for 5 minutes. Take the cinnamon out, and serve the curry hot, with rice.

Pecan pie (USA)

Pecan nuts are an important crop for farmers in the southern USA. They **export** them all over the world. Pecan nuts have a sweeter flavour than most nuts. Pecan pie is a popular traditional dish all over the USA. It is delicious warm or cold.

What you need

50g dark soft brown sugar

4 tbsp golden syrup

1 tbsp butter

18cm shortcrust pastry flan case

200g pecan halves

1 egg

1 tsp vanilla essence

What you do

 1 Put the sugar, golden syrup, and butter into a pan. Heat them very gently over a low heat until the butter has **melted**. Stir well and leave to **cool**.

 2 **Preheat** the oven to 180°C/350°F/gas mark 4.

 3 Put the pastry case on to a baking sheet.

 4 Scatter half the pecans over the pastry, and level them. Arrange a circle of pecan halves around the edge of the pastry, and then another circle inside it. Keep making circles of nuts until you reach the centre.

 5 **Beat** the egg and the vanilla essence with a fork. Stir this into the cooled sugar mixture, and then pour the liquid over the pecan nuts.

6 **Bake** the pie for 30 minutes, or until the egg and sugar mixture has set in the centre of the pie. Cool for 15 minutes.

7 Cut the pie into six slices, and serve with ice cream or cream.

THE HISTORY OF PECAN PIE

In the late seventeenth century, French explorers settled in New Orleans, USA. The Native Americans living there introduced them to the pecan nut. The French settlers invented pecan pie – a delicious way to enjoy the nuts.

Apple pancakes (The Netherlands)

People in the Netherlands enjoy sweet and savoury pancakes. They might cook them with cheese, ham, or fruit. Traditionally, Dutch cooks do not roll their pancakes up around the filling. Instead, they cook the filling with the batter, and serve the pancake flat on a large plate. This recipe is a particularly popular one in the Netherlands.

What you need

100g plain flour
2 tsp soft brown sugar
1 tsp **ground** cinnamon
¼ tsp ground cloves
1 egg
200ml milk
1 red apple
1 green apple
4 tsp vegetable oil

What you do

 Sift the flour, sugar, and ground spices into a bowl. Using your fingers, make a dip in the middle.

 In a separate bowl, **beat** the egg. Add the milk and beat until well mixed. Pour the mixture into the dip in the flour, and gradually stir the liquid into the flour.

3 Beat the pancake batter well, and then put it on one side. Turn the oven on to its lowest setting.

 Cut the apples in half and remove the cores. **Slice** the apples thinly.

5 Stir the apple slices into the batter.

6 Heat ¼ tsp oil in an 18cm frying pan. Using a metal tablespoon, add 2 tablespoons of pancake batter and apple slices to the pan. Tilt the pan to cover the bottom with batter.

7 Cook for 2–3 minutes over a low to medium heat, until the pancake is golden brown on one side.

8 Use a **fish slice** to flip the pancake over, and cook the other side. Lift the pancake on to a plate, **cover** it, and keep it warm in the oven while you cook the rest of the batter in the same way.

9 Serve the pancakes hot, either on their own, or with a little golden syrup or ice cream.

Athol brosse (Scotland)

Athol brosse means "broth, or thick soup, from Athol", which is an area in Scotland. The main ingredients are all produced in Scotland – oatmeal, honey, and raspberries. Serve Athol brosse as a dessert, or as a cool treat on a hot day.

What you need

6 tbsp pinhead oatmeal
450ml double cream
3 tbsp runny honey
200g fresh raspberries
Sprigs of mint

What you do

1 Scatter the oatmeal on to a grill pan.

2 Heat the grill to medium. **Grill** the oatmeal for about 1 minute, until the oatmeal starts to turn golden brown. Set it aside to **cool**.

3 Put the cream into a bowl and **whisk** it until it starts becoming firmer.

4 Spoon the honey over the cream.

5 Tip the oatmeal into the cream. Using a metal spoon, cut through the cream to **fold** it in.

Ready to eat: 55 minutes (including 30 minutes to chill the mixture).
Difficulty: *. Serves 4.

6 Keeping four raspberries aside, divide the rest up into four glass bowls. Spoon the cream mixture on top of the raspberries.

7 Top each glass with a raspberry and a sprig of fresh mint.

8 **Chill** for 30 minutes before serving.

HEATHER HONEY
Bees collect pollen from flowers to make into honey. The bees that make Scottish honey have gathered pollen from the heather flowers that cover the hills and mountains of Scotland. Scots say that this makes their honey taste unlike any other kind.

Further Information

Here are some places to find out more about **vegetarian** food and cooking.

Books

Cooking With Herb: The Vegetarian Dragon by Jules Bass
   (Barefoot Books, 2009)

The Jumbo Vegetarian Cookbook by Judi Gillies and Jennifer Glossop
   (Kids Can Press, 2008)

The Vegan Lunchbox by Jennifer McCann (De Capo Lifelong, 2008)

Vegetarian Food by Susannah Blake (Wayland, 2008)

The Vegetarian Kids' Cookbook: Fresh, Fun Food by Roz Denny (Lorenz, 2009)

Websites

www.spatulatta.com/vegetarian.html

www.theveggietable.com/recipes/recipes-kids.html

http://kidsarevegantoo.blogspot.com/2006/09/vegan-recipes-for-kids.html

www.parsleysoup.co.uk/list php?category=kids

Healthy eating

This diagram shows the types and proportion of food you should eat to stay healthy. Eat plenty of foods from the *bread, rice, potatoes, pasta* group and plenty from the *fruit and vegetables* group. Eat some foods from the *milk and dairy* group and the *meat, fish, eggs, beans* group. Foods from the smallest group are not necessary for a healthy diet so eat these in small amounts or only occasionally.

↑ The Eatwell food plate shows the proportion of food from each food group you should eat to achieve a healthy, balanced diet. This takes account of everything you eat, including snacks.

Glossary

bake cook something in the oven

beat mix something together strongly using a fork, spoon, or whisk

blend mix ingredients together in a blender or food processor

boil cook a liquid on the hob. Boiling liquid bubbles and steams strongly.

calcium mineral in foods, such as milk and cheese, that helps us have strong teeth and bones

chill put something in the fridge to make it cold before serving it

chop cut something into pieces using a knife

colander bowl-shaped container with holes in it, used for draining vegetables and straining

cool allow hot food to become cold. You should always allow food to cool before putting it in the fridge.

cover put a lid on a pan, or foil over a dish

deep-fried cooked in a deep, hot oil

dice cut into cubes

drain remove liquid, usually by pouring something into a colander or sieve

dressing oil and vinegar sauce for salad

export sell a product, such as fruit, to another country

fish slice utensil for lifting fish or other fried food out of a pan. It is like a flat spoon with slits in it.

fold mix ingredients together very slowly and carefully

fry cook something in oil in a pan

grate break something such as cheese into small pieces, using a grater

grill cook something under the grill

ground made into a fine powder

mash crush something such as potatoes until it is soft and pulpy

melt change from solid to liquid when heated

nutrient substance that provides nourishment

peel remove the skin of a fruit or vegetable

pitta bread flat, unrisen bread

preheat turn on the oven or grill in advance, so that it is hot when you want to use it

protein a body-building material found in some foods, such as beans, eggs, and meat

pulse beans, peas, or seeds from plants that often have pods

rinse wash under a cold tap

season give extra flavour to food by adding salt or pepper

sift pass flour or other powder through a sieve

simmer cook liquid on the hob. Simmering liquid bubbles and steams gently.

slice cut something into thin, flat pieces

sprinkle scatter small pieces or drops on to something

staple main food in a diet

thaw defrost something that has been frozen

toast heat in a pan without any oil

toss turn the leaves in a salad over a few times so they are coated in dressing

vegan person who does not eat any food that has come from an animal, including milk and eggs

vegetarian food that does not contain meat or fish. People who don't eat meat or fish are called vegetarians.

vitamins natural chemicals in food that the body uses to stay healthy

whisk mix ingredients using a whisk

Index